KT-494-947

Words printed in **bold** are explained
in the glossary.

Acknowledgments
The publishers would like to thank Wendy Body for acting as
reading level consultant and Robin Kerrod as factual adviser.

Photographic credits
Page 41, Airship Industries Ltd; front endpapers and title page,
Allsport/Simon Bruty; page 18, Allsport/Russell Cheyne; page 19,
Allsport/Mike Powell; page 29, Allsport/Vandystadt; page 24,
British Rail InterCity; pages 27 (bottom), 42 and 43, J Allan Cash;
page 40, Rex Features; page 9, Ford Motor Company; page 23,
Colin Garratt; pages 6, 7, 11 (top), 20, 25, 31 (top), 35, 39 and 41
(top), Robert Harding Picture Library; page 17, JCB Sales Ltd;
page 27 (top), Mansell Collection; page 22 (top), National
Railway Museum, York; pages 14 and 15 (top), Scania (Great
Britain) Ltd; page 13 (top), Science Photo Library; pages 13 and
30-31, Shell (UK) Ltd; page 43 (top), Spacecharts; pages 11
(bottom), 15 (bottom), 37 and 40 (bottom), ZEFA.

Designed by R W Ditchfield.

Vehicles

written by ANITA GANERI
illustrated by JEREMY GOWER

Ladybird

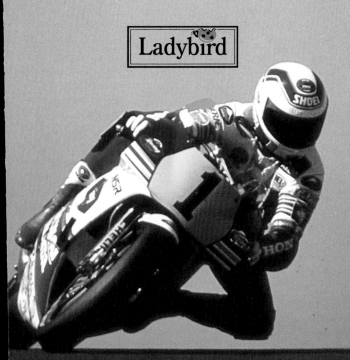

Getting about

Every day we use many different types of transport. Cars, trains, ships and planes take us to work, school and on holiday. They also carry **cargo** from place to place.

In the past, people used animals and simple forms of transport like rowing boats.

ancient coracle

sedan chair

horse-drawn cart with wooden wheels

Cargo can be letters and parcels, food, machines and even animals.

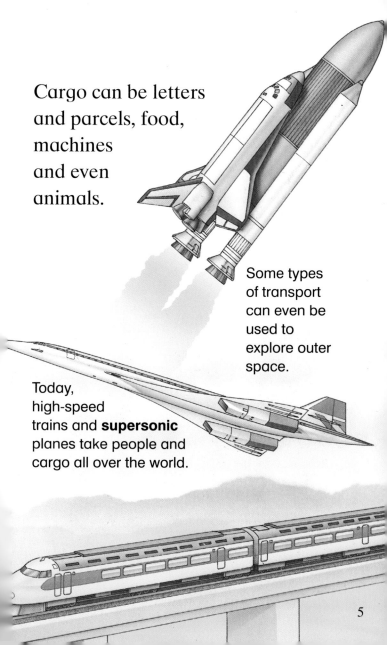

Some types of transport can even be used to explore outer space.

Today, high-speed trains and **supersonic** planes take people and cargo all over the world.

Animal transport

Animals used to be the main form of transport before **engines** were invented. They pulled cartloads of goods and carriages of people.

Camels are probably the best way of getting about in hot, sandy deserts. Their wide feet keep a firm grip on the soft, loose sand.

In the Arctic and Antarctic, husky dogs are used to pull sledges along. The dogs are very strong and have thick coats to protect them from the bitter cold.

In some parts of the world, animals are still used for transport.

Water buffaloes are often used to pull the farmer's plough through rice fields.

Cars

Modern cars have over 20,000 different parts all working together to make the car move. Most cars are built in special factories. The car goes through the factory and parts are added to it one by one.

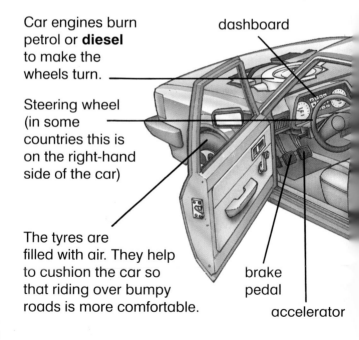

Car engines burn petrol or **diesel** to make the wheels turn.

dashboard

Steering wheel (in some countries this is on the right-hand side of the car)

The tyres are filled with air. They help to cushion the car so that riding over bumpy roads is more comfortable.

brake pedal

accelerator

The body of the car is made from large sheets of metal cut into shape by machines. The engine and other working parts inside are fixed to a steel frame. Sometimes the body and frame are built in one piece.

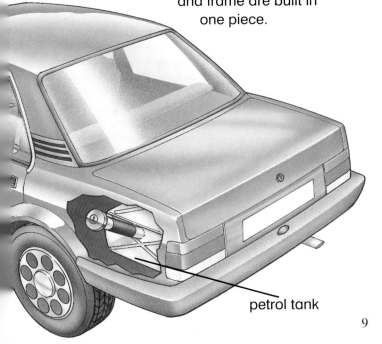

petrol tank

Built for speed

Racing cars are built to go much faster than family cars. Formula One cars are the fastest racers. They are low and light with a powerful engine so they can speed round the track easily.

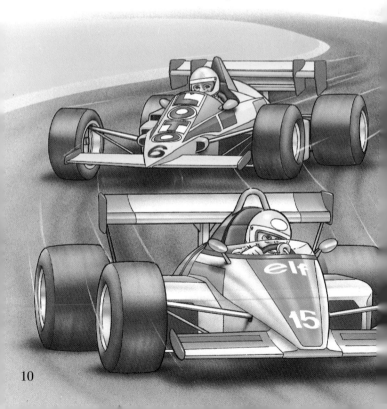

The cars reach over 290 km per hour on the straight parts of the track and up to 150 km per hour round the corners. Drivers need to be very skilful to keep control.

During a race the tyres wear out very quickly and may need to be changed several times. It takes a racing team only about eight seconds to change all four tyres.

Thrust 2 (below) is the fastest car in the world. In 1983 it travelled at over 1000 km per hour.

Special cars

Today, many people are worried that the petrol used to power cars is poisoning the air. In some big cities, traffic fumes and fog mix together to make thick, harmful smog.

Solar-powered cars are covered in **solar panels**. These panels collect sunlight and change it into electricity, which turns the car's wheels.

Other ways to power cars are now being tried out.

Electric cars are clean and quiet, but their batteries soon go flat and have to be charged. To do this a special cable is linked up to an electricity supply.

This car has been designed to run on very little fuel. It can travel for over 1000 km on just one litre of petrol.

Lorries

Lorries carry cargo, such as food, bricks and cars, from one place to another. They have strong steel bodies and large wheels, often in pairs, to support their loads.

Small lorries are called rigid vehicles and are built in one piece. The driver's cab is attached to a flat trailer or container for the goods.

Larger lorries are built in several sections so that they can bend to go round corners. These vehicles are called articulated lorries and can carry loads weighing over 50 tonnes.

Lorries can be adapted for special uses. Some have cranes or scoops for work on building sites and in quarries.

Four-wheel drive

Jeeps, Land Rovers and pick-up trucks are specially made for driving over sand, snow and even through water.

Land Rovers were first built in 1948. Today they are often used on expeditions up mountains, across deserts and even over ice in the Antarctic. They have tough aluminium bodies and powerful engines.

They are called four-wheel drive vehicles because the engine makes all four wheels turn, instead of just two as on an ordinary car. This gives the driver better control and makes driving safer over rough ground.

Four-wheel drive diggers can move easily over loose or muddy ground to clear earth and rubble from building sites.

Bicycles

Bicycles are a quick and clean form of transport. The rider pushes on the pedals, which turn a cog wheel and chain to make the back wheel go round.

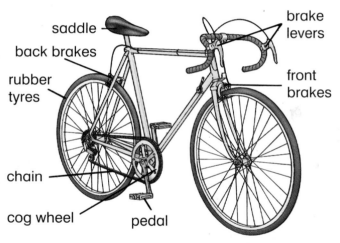

saddle

back brakes

rubber tyres

chain

cog wheel

pedal

brake levers

front brakes

Racing bikes have very light frames and wheels so that they can go faster.

Mountain bikes have strong tyres with grooves so that they can grip rocky or bumpy ground.

One of the most famous bikes was the penny farthing. It had a huge front wheel and a much smaller back wheel. There was a step built onto the frame to help the rider to get up. Falling off was easy!

Motorbikes

The first motorbikes were pedal bikes fitted with steam engines. The rider had to push the bike to get the engine started.

In sidecar racing, a seat is fitted to the side of a motorbike. As the bike goes round corners, the passenger leans right out to keep it well balanced.

The size of the engine of a modern motorbike is measured in cubic centimetres (cc). The bigger the engine, the more powerful it is.

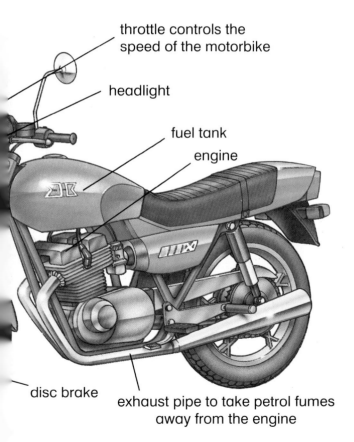

throttle controls the speed of the motorbike

headlight

fuel tank

engine

disc brake

exhaust pipe to take petrol fumes away from the engine

Steam trains

Trains were first used over 160
years ago to carry people and
cargo from place to place.
The early trains were pulled
by engines or **locomotives**,
powered by steam.

A copy of the *Rocket*,
one of the earliest steam
locomotives. It was built
by an Englishman,
George Stephenson,
in 1829.

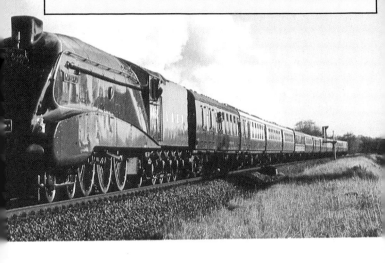

The *Mallard* was the fastest ever steam locomotive. In 1938 it set a record speed of over 200 km per hour.

Steam locomotives burned coal or wood in a fire, which heated up a tank of water. The steam from the boiling water moved cylinders called pistons, which pushed the wheels round. Steam trains still run today in a few parts of the world.

Diesel and electric trains

Most trains today are pulled by diesel or electric locomotives. They can go much faster than steam trains and are more comfortable to ride in.

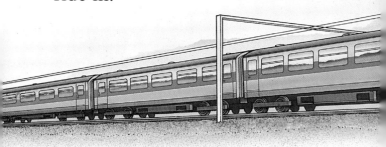

British Rail's *InterCity 125* is the fastest diesel train in the world. It has a top speed of 233 km per hour.

Electric trains pick up electricity from overhead cables or from a special rail on the ground.

The fastest train in the world is an electric train, the French **TGV**. It can reach an amazing top speed of 515 km per hour.

Going underground

Many big cities around the world have underground railways. Underground trains run on electricity that they pick up from a track on the ground.

The New York subway has over 450 stations – more than any other underground railway.

Some trains are automatic. As the train goes over certain spots on the track, electronic signals make the train slow down or speed up.

The first underground railway was opened in London. The first underground trains had steam powered engines.

The world's busiest underground is in Moscow. It carries over six million passengers every day.

Sailing boats

Sailing boats have carried people and cargo for thousands of years. Sailing ships also made it possible for explorers such as Christopher Columbus to discover new parts of the world far from their homes.

The mainsail is moved by swinging the boom.

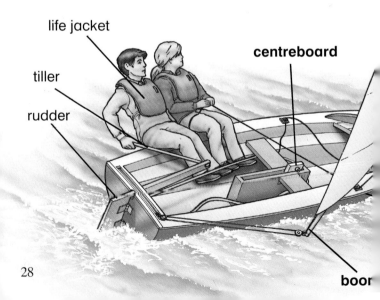

life jacket

centreboard

tiller

rudder

boom

Modern sailing boats have triangular sails with a curved edge, designed to catch the wind. The force of the wind pushes against the sails and moves the boat along. The tiller moves the rudder to change the direction.

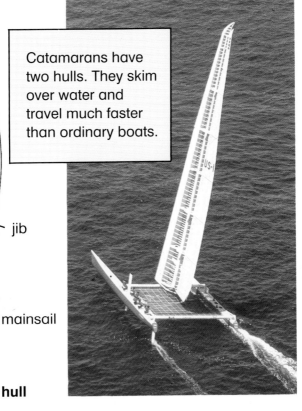

Catamarans have two hulls. They skim over water and travel much faster than ordinary boats.

jib

mainsail

hull

Liners and cargo ships

Liners and cargo ships are huge boats that travel all over the world. People used to travel on liners to other countries, before planes made long-distance travel much quicker. Today most liners are used as floating hotels to take passengers on holiday cruises.

The largest cargo ships carry oil. These supertankers are too big to go right into the docks to unload, so the oil is pumped into storage tanks outside the docks.

The *Queen Elizabeth 2* is the biggest passenger liner under the British Flag used today. She has over 900 cabins, a cinema, shops and restaurants, tennis courts and swimming pools.

Submarines

Submarines can travel under water
and ice. Their engines use diesel
oil or nuclear power to turn a
propeller at the back, which drives
the submarine forward.

crew quarters

Hydroplanes help
to direct the
submarine as it goes
underwater or rises
to the surface.

(1)

Nuclear-powered submarines can
stay under water for about two
years without having to come to
the surface.

ballast
tanks

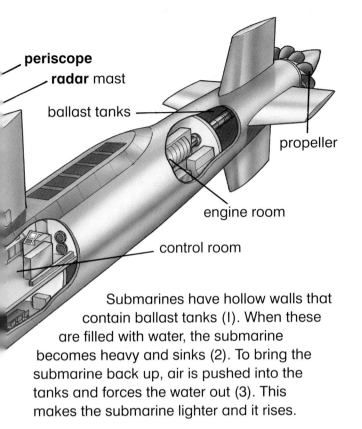

periscope

radar mast

ballast tanks

propeller

engine room

control room

Submarines have hollow walls that contain ballast tanks (I). When these are filled with water, the submarine becomes heavy and sinks (2). To bring the submarine back up, air is pushed into the tanks and forces the water out (3). This makes the submarine lighter and it rises.

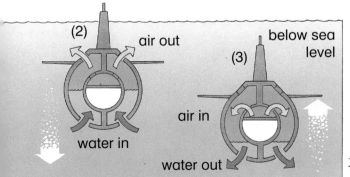

(2) air out

below sea level

(3)

air in

water in

water out

33

Hovercraft and hydrofoils

Hovercraft are often used on short sea crossings because they can go faster than ordinary boats. They sit on a huge cushion of air covered by a rubber skirt that stops the air escaping.

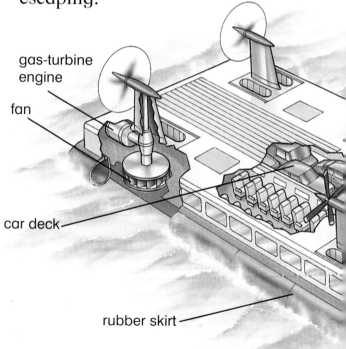

gas-turbine engine

fan

car deck

rubber skirt

Gas-turbine engines turn huge air propellers that push the boat forwards and it skims across the surface of the water.

Hydrofoils have special underwater wings. As the boat picks up speed, the wings rise up and lift the boat out of the water. Then the boat skims across the water on its wings, rather like a water-skier.

air propellers

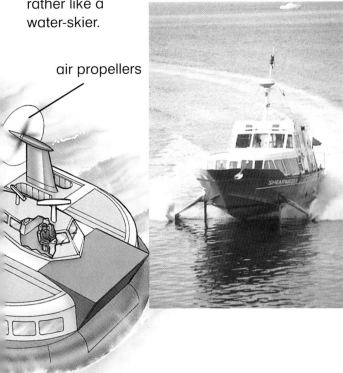

Aeroplanes

Modern aeroplanes have powerful jet engines and can fly very fast. Jet engines use a fuel called **kerosene**. As kerosene burns, it makes hot gases, which rush out of the back of the engine and move the plane forwards.

The largest passenger plane in the world is the *Boeing* 747 or 'Jumbo' jet. It can carry up to 567 people and fly at over 900 km per hour.

jet engines

The fastest passenger plane is the supersonic *Concorde*. It cruises at 2,333 km per hour and can fly between London and New York in only three hours.

Aeroplane wings are specially shaped so that air pushes up underneath them to keep the plane in the sky.

fuel tank inside wing

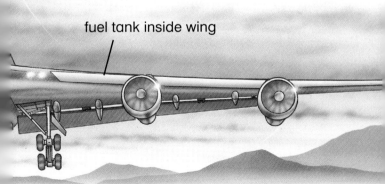

Helicopters

Most aircraft have to take off and land from a long runway. Helicopters can take off and land vertically (straight up or down). Instead of wings, helicopters have rotor blades that spin round very fast to lift the aircraft.

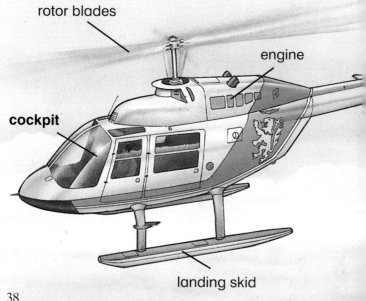

rotor blades

engine

cockpit

landing skid

The **pilot** can tilt the blades to make the helicopter go forwards, backwards or sidewards. Helicopters can also **hover** in one place.

The biggest helicopter in the world is the former Russian *Mil Mi-12*. It weighs over 100 tonnes and has four powerful engines to turn its blades.

tail rotor controls movement from left to right

Helicopters are used to rescue people in trouble at sea.

Hot-air balloons and airships

Hot-air balloons were invented by the Montgolfier brothers in 1783. Hot air is blown into the balloon to make it rise and then kept hot by bursts of flame.

Montgolfier balloon

Balloons cannot be steered. They go where the wind blows them.

The gases helium and hydrogen are also used to fill balloons. Both these gases are lighter than air.

Airships are balloons fitted with engines and propellers so that they can be steered. Today, small airships called blimps are used for advertising and filming sports matches for television.

Travels in space

In the past, a journey of a few kilometres could take many hours. Today, in a spacecraft, people can travel nearly 30,000 km in an hour.

The American space shuttle is a special rocket because it can be used again and again. It takes off like an ordinary rocket but comes in to land on a runway like a plane.

On 21st July 1969 the American **astronaut** Neil Armstrong became the first man to walk on the Moon. He landed on the surface in a lunar module, a special vehicle that was part of the *Apollo 11* spacecraft.

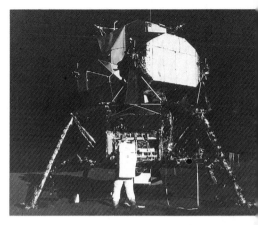

In 1971 the *Apollo 15* crew took a special space car to the Moon. It was called a lunar rover. The astronauts used it when they collected rocks and soil and took photographs of the Moon's surface.

Glossary

astronaut A human being who travels in space. Another word for astronaut is cosmonaut.

boom A pole attached at one end to a mast to stretch the bottom of a sail.

cargo Goods carried by ship, aircraft or vehicle.

centreboard A movable board that can be dropped down under the hull to stop a boat drifting sideways.

cockpit The area where the pilot sits to control an aircraft.

diesel A type of oil used as fuel in diesel engines.

engine A machine that uses fuel, such as petrol or electricity, to make something move.

hover To stay in the air in one place.

hull The body of a ship.

kerosene An oil used for burning in jet engines (also called paraffin).

locomotive A railway engine.

periscope A pole with a mirror at both ends that allows sailors in submarines to see above the water, while remaining hidden underwater.

pilot A person who flies an aircraft or guides ships in and out of a harbour.

propeller A set of specially shaped blades that spin round to drive aircraft and ships.

radar A way of finding distant objects, such as ships and aircraft, by using radio waves.

solar panel A flat object that collects sunlight and turns it into electricity.

supersonic Faster than the speed of sound.

TGV *Train à Grande Vitesse* – French for 'high-speed train'.